Michael M. Dediu

World Constitution

With Lovely Comments

Moving from many suboptimal
constitutions to the much better
Constitution of the World

DERC Publishing House

Nashua, New Hampshire, U. S. A.

Published and printed in the
United States of America
On the Great Seal of the United States are included:
E Pluribus Unum (Out of many, one)
Annuit Coeptis (He has approved of the undertakings)
Novus Ordo Seclorum (New order of the ages)

Library of Congress Control Number: 2020915195

Dediu, Michael M.

World Constitution with Lovely Comments
Moving from many suboptimal constitutions to the much better
Constitution of the World

ISBN-13: 978-1-950999-19-4

MSG0444024_PqpDCkGP26oda6pkX53l
MSG0444146_f1w0c1B1b6aEIA3kKmEx

Preface

There are many suboptimal constitutions in the world, and people ask for a much better one – The Constitution of the World. We added some lovely comments to this Constitution of the World, to be better understood, and easier to implement by the people.

The third president of the United States, Thomas Jefferson, said about 175 years ago, in 1825: "I know no safe depository of the ultimate powers of the society but the people themselves. This is the true corrective of abuses of constitutional power."

Churchill, over 60 years ago, said that "If the human race wishes to have a prolonged and indefinite period of material prosperity, they have only got to behave in a peaceful and helpful way toward one another".

In this book we develop these ideas and other new ideas, commenting on the new Constitution of the World, which will create the conditions for a peaceful, free and prosperous new country, Peaceful Terra.

The future begins to take shape, and looks really great!

Michael M. Dediu, Ph. D.

Nashua, New Hampshire, U. S. A., 11 August 2020

USA, Bretton Woods: The Gold Room in the Mount Washington Resort (1902, elevation 500 m, by Joseph Stickney (1840 – 1903, coal business)), where the documents of the United Nations Monetary and Financial Conference (1 – 22 July 1944, 730 delegates from 44 Allied nations, at Bretton Woods (12 km west of Mount Washington (1917 m), 250 km north of Boston), established the International Monetary Fund and the World Bank. The Bretton Woods system worked for 27 years, until 1971) were signed. On the right - a table with the flags of the 44 Allied nations.

Table of Contents

UK, London: From the Bow Street, the northeast façade of the Royal Opera House at Covent Garden (1732, 1808, 1858, 1999, capacity 2,256). In 1734, Covent Garden presented its first ballet, Pygmalion. On 14 January 1947, the Covent Garden Opera Company gave its first performance of Carmen (1875, opera in four acts, based on a novella of the same title by Prosper Mérimée (1803-1870 (age 67))) by French composer Georges Bizet (1838-1875 (age 36)).

The Constitution of the World

SUN: Tell me, how does this important Constitution start?

EARTH: It starts with an introductory statement:

Proposition 1. We, the People of the World

We, the People on this Earth, in order to
    1.1 - completely eliminate war and any type of conflicts,
    1.2 - have a peaceful and harmonious world,
    1.3 - have freedom, dignity, good families and respect,
    1.4 - have good health and good education,
    1.5 - have a friendly atmosphere and prosperity,
    1.6 – have the safety and wellbeing of all the people in the world as the highest priority,
    1.7 – use the best peaceful results, experience and knowledge of all current countries,

establish this Constitution of the World.

SUN: It is immediately noticeable that the first priority is the elimination of war and any type of conflicts.

EARTH: Yes, indeed, and building on this we'll have a peaceful and harmonious world, freedom, dignity, good families and respect.

SUN: Do you remember what James Madison said about 190 years ago?

EARTH: Certainly: "The means of defense agst. foreign danger, have been always the instruments of tyranny at home."
"The advancement and diffusion of knowledge is the only guardian of true liberty."

SUN: Then, naturally, good health and good education are high priorities.

EARTH: Nice to see that the safety and wellbeing of all the people in the world is mentioned as the highest priority.

SUN: How do you achieve all these really good objectives?

EARTH: Certainly, it will be necessary to use the best peaceful results, experience and knowledge of all current countries.

USA, Bretton Woods: The table with the flags of the 44 Allied nations, which attended the United Nations Monetary and Financial Conference in July 1944, in the Gold Room of the Mount Washington Resort (1902).

Proposition 2. Peaceful Terra

2.1 - All the people of the world will be proud citizens of only one country, called Peaceful Terra, with total area of over 509 M km^2, and land area over 148 M km^2.

2.2 - All the rules – not more than 2,000, on maximum 1,000 pages - on our Earth will be established by the people and their elected Advisers.

SUN: What's new in this Proposition 2?

EARTH: Everything: first - all the people of the world will be proud citizens of only one country, called Peaceful Terra.

SUN: No more lots of conflicting countries. And second?

EARTH: Limitation on rules - not more than 2,000, on maximum 1,000 pages. And all the rules on our Earth will be established by the people and their elected Advisers, not separate institutions just for making laws ad infinitum.

SUN: You remember Churchill…

EARTH: "If you have ten thousand regulations you destroy all respect for the law."

USA, New York: On 7th Avenue at West 57th Street, looking southwest: right: a classical building, which is tangent to the right, on W 57th St, to the American Fine Arts Society building (1892); left down: a beautiful building, opposite Carnegie Hall (to the left, across 7th Ave, 1891, concert hall with exceptional acoustics, architecture and performance history); left up: an impressive double skyscraper, with the southwest side on W 56th St.

Proposition 3. Ten Simple and Friendly Regions

3.1 - For easier administration, Peaceful Terra will be only administratively divided in 10 simple and friendly regions of around 770 M people each, called R0, R1,…, R9, which will be delimited by meridians (or line of longitudes), with the assistance of the United Nations.

3.2 - Each region will have a pair of capitals plus an outside city, for better and more homogenous management (all will change every year; more details are in the annex book "World with One Country & its Ten Friendly Regions - Moving from 195 disagreeing countries, to 1 country with 10 collaborating regions"). For example, the first implementation will be:

R0 between meridians 0 and 15^0 E, capitals: Bern (Switzerland), Libreville (Gabon), and Oxford (UK).

R1: 15^0 E - 30^0 E, Warsaw (Poland), Pretoria (South Africa) and Miami (FL, USA).

R2: 30^0 E - 45^0 E, Moscow (Russia), Cairo (Egypt), and Grenoble (France).

R3: 45^0 E - 75^0 E, Astana (Kazakhstan), Karachi (Pakistan), and Montpellier (France).

R4: 75^0 E - 85^0 E, New Delhi (India), Novosibirsk (Russia), and Magdeburg (Germany).

R5: 85^0 E - 100^0 E, Krasnoyarsk (Russia), Urumqi (China), and Avignon (France).

R6: 100^0 E - 115^0 E, Jakarta (Indonesia), Beijing (China), and Neuchâtel (Switzerland).

R7: 115^0 E - 180^0, Tokyo (Japan), Sydney (Australia), and Malmö (Sweden).

R8: 180^0 - 70^0 Washington (USA), Mexico City (Mexico), and Bellinzona (Switzerland).

R9: 70^0 W – 0 Halifax (Canada), Brasilia (Brazil), and Biel (Switzerland).

SUN: This Proposition 3 brings numerous significant changes.

EARTH: Yes, 10 simple and friendly administrative regions of around 770 M people each, called R0, R1,…, R9, delimited by meridians, are really good and helpful for people, because they will promptly receive help, when necessary, from the World Government.

SUN: It is really nice to have all these cities collaborating.

EARTH: Indeed, this atmosphere of friendship and collaboration is the essence of the new one country on Earth concept.
Seneca is with us: One of the most beautiful qualities of true friendship is to understand and to be understood.

USA, Washington (1790), National Gallery of Art (1937, National Mall)

3.2. Each of the 10 regions will be divided by meridians in 10 sub-regions S00,   , S99, each with about 77 M people.

3.3. Each of the 100 sub-regions will be divided in 10 districts D000, D001,   , D999, each with about 7.7 M people, and each of the districts will have their current small and big cities.

SUN: 100 subregions and 1,000 districts on Earth looks great.

EARTH: They will help distribute the top-level money and decisions to the people, and to receive from the people their comments and observations.

3.4. Having telework, many people will have a northern residence and a southern residence, seasonally moving from one to the other, to avoid extreme cold or heat, and having the same hour.

SUN: Northern residences and southern residences are interesting.

EARTH: Yes, it creates mobility, people can enjoy good weather all year around, and, most importantly, people will meet and collaborate with each other.

3.5. All the oceans will belong to some of the regions defined above, therefore will be maintained by those regions, to be free of any piracy or other bad activity – World Police will help when necessary.

SUN: The oceans play an important role.

EARTH: Indeed, and now, for the first time, all oceans will belong to one country, therefore all people will have free access and free use of the oceans – this will certainly create a great increase in commerce, travel and good life for all.

Newton also mentions the great ocean of truth: I do not know what I may appear to the world; but to myself I seem to have been only like a boy playing on the seashore, and diverting myself now and then finding a smoother pebble or a prettier shell than ordinary, whilst the great ocean of truth lay all undiscovered before me.

UK, London: The northeast exterior of Paul Hamlyn Hall (old Covent Garden flower market), southeast of the Royal Opera House (right

Proposition 4. No borders

4.1 - In Peaceful Terra there are no borders.

SUN: This is a big dream!

EARTH: For thousands of years people dreamed about not having borders – now, finally, this dream is reality.

4.2 - There will be just simple administrative delimitations, and all these delimitations between regions, as well as between sub-regions, will be flexible – they will be changed after each census (5 years), for maintaining a balanced number of people in all regions (around 770 M) and sub-regions (around 77 M).

4.3 - In the first implementation presented in Proposition 3, there are many big differences between the populations of different regions, and then between the populations of different sub-regions, but this is just the first implementation, which needs to be quickly put in place, and then, very easily, the delimitations will be moved a few kilometers east or west, to reach a balanced population.

4.4 - Because all the people are in the same country, it is normal to modify a little its regions, for better administration, to make everybody happy.

4.5 - It is well understood that there will be some difficulties in the beginning, like in all beginnings, but with calm, patience, perseverance and hard work, the things will improve fast, and all the people will enjoy a better life.

SUN: Flexible delimitations look good.

EARTH: Yes, to eliminate big differences between regions, it is really great to change these delimitations after each census (5 years). These changes will be mostly in computers, and people will benefit having better services from the government. For example, the driver license will be valid everywhere, no need to change it like now, when even inside one country (like the U.S.), if you move a few kilometers, from a state to another state, you need a lot of bureaucracy to change the driver license. The same story for the car inspection. All this wasted time, money and energy will be used to improve people's lives.

UK, London: Inside the Covent Garden Market, with an opera soprano performing (center right down).

Proposition 5. The Government of Peaceful Terra

5.1. The family of over 7. 7 B people

from Peaceful Terra will have four levels of world management; at the local level, if needed, it could be one or two more levels of local managers (mayors, town managers, county managers – all levels of management must be friendly, helpful, fast, polite, modest and smart):

5.2. Level 1 Management: 1,000 L1 friendly managers

1,000 L1 friendly managers for the 1,000 districts, who will supervise and assist the mayors and town managers from their district, for a total of about 7,700,000 people in each district. Each of the 1,000 L1 friendly managers will be located in a central city from their districts – they could be the mayors of those cities, but with new responsibilities for the whole district.

SUN: Nice to see the emphasis on friendliness at the local level.

EARTH: Yes, sometimes the local government are not as friendly as they should be, and now we'll see a big change in better.

5.3. Level 2 Management: 100 L2 friendly managers

100 L2 friendly managers for the 100 sub-regions, who will supervise and assist the 10 L1 managers of the 10 districts of each sub-region, for a total of about 77,000,000 people for each sub-region. These 100 L2 friendly managers will move each month between the two capitals of each of the 100 sub-regions.

USA, New York: On West 42nd Street at Fifth Avenue, looking southeast at Chrysler building (back up, Walter P. Chrysler (1875-1940), 1930, 319 m, 77 floors, 111,000 m^2 floor area, 32 elevators, at Lexington Avenue), before it is Grand Hyatt New York Hotel (1919, 90 m), and before it is Grand Central Terminal (1871, 1903, 1913, 2000, built by Cornelius Vanderbilt (1794-1877, the 2nd richest American, after John D. Rockefeller (1839-1937)) and his 13 children, commuter railroad terminal, with a grand façade and concourse, at Park Avenue, 47 acres, 44 high-level platforms, 67 tracks on 2 levels).

In the beginning these capitals will be:

In Region R0: from Paris (France) to N'Djamena (Chad)

- The sub-region R00 will have the capitals Paris (France) and Niamey (Niger) – assistance from Magdeburg (Germany).
- The sub-region R01 will have the capitals Brussels (Belgium) and Porto-Novo (Benin) - assistance from Toronto (Canada).
- The sub-region R02 will have the capitals Amsterdam (Netherlands) and Algiers (Algeria) - assistance from Graz (Austria).
- The sub-region R03 will have the capitals Luxembourg (Luxembourg) and Sao Tome (Sao Tome and Principe) - assistance from Adelaide (Australia).
- The sub-region R04 will have the capitals of Abuja (Nigeria) and Bochum (Germany) - assistance from Nikko (Japan).
- The sub-region R05 will have the capitals Malabo (Equatorial Guinea), and Zürich (Switzerland) - assistance from Leeds (UK).
- The sub-region R06 will have the capitals Oslo (Norway) and Tunis (Tunisia) - assistance from Sheffield (UK).
- The sub-region R07 will have the capitals Roma (Italy) and Luanda (Angola) - assistance from Yamagata (Japan).
- The sub-region R08 will have the capitals in Berlin (Germany) and Tripoli (Libya) - assistance from New York (USA).
- The sub-region R09 will have the capitals Prague (Czech Republic) and N'Djamena (Chad) - assistance from Brisbane (Australia).

SUN: There are many great cities here.

EARTH: And they will work with smaller cities, to have a better understanding of different groups of people, for better assistance to all people of each sub-region.

Rome: Center: Columna Traiani (113 AD) with a band (180 m) of carved reliefs, which winds around the Trajan's Column, regarding Trajan's Dacian war campaigns (101-102 and 105-106 AD). After Trajan's death, his 6 m statue was on top until 1587. His ashes and later those of his wife Plotina were placed in the base of the column. Left: Santissimo Nome di Maria al Foro Traiano (1751, the Church of the Most Holy Name of Mary at the Trajan Forum).

In Region R1: from Zagreb (Croatia) to Bujumbura (Burundi)

- The sub-region R10 will have the capitals in Zagreb (Croatia) and Brazzaville (Congo) - assistance from Nantes (France).
- The sub-region R11 will have the capitals in Vienna (Austria), Windhoek (Namibia) - assistance from Bilbao (Spain).
- The sub-region R12 will have the capitals in Stockholm (Sweden), Bangui (Central African Republic) - assistance from Florence (Italy).
- The sub-region R13 will have the capitals in Budapest (Hungary), Rundu (Namibia) - assistance from Monaco (Monaco).
- The sub-region R14 will have the capitals in Belgrade (Serbia), Kananga (Democratic Republic of Congo) - assistance from Liverpool (UK).
- The sub-region R15 will have the capitals in Athens (Greece), Mongu (Zambia) - assistance from Los Angeles (CA, USA).
- The sub-region R16 will have the capitals in Helsinki (Finland) and Kolwezi (Democratic Republic of the Congo) - assistance from Montreal (Canada).
- The sub-region R17 will have the capitals in Bucharest (Romania) and Gaborone (Botswana) - assistance from Philadelphia (PA, USA).
- The sub-region R18 will have the capitals in Minsk (Belarus) and Maseru (Lesotho) - assistance from Orleans (France).
- The sub-region R19 will have the capitals in Chisinau (Republic of Moldova) and Bujumbura (Burundi) - assistance from Hamburg (Germany).

SUN: Let's see, the enjoyable sub-region R16 will have the capitals in Helsinki (Finland) and?

EARTH: Kolwezi (Democratic Republic of the Congo) – it was a typo in a previous edition of the Constitution, and we apologize. The good news is that these capitals will frequently change, for the benefit of all people.

USA: The George Washington Bridge (1962, 1450 m, spanning Hudson River from New York City to Fort Lee, New Jersey, with routes 95 and 80, near Exit 73 for Fort Lee and route 67.

USA, New York: W 42nd Street, near 8th Avenue, with the Chrysler Building (1930, 320 m, 77 floors, center-right far back).

In Region R2: from Kiev (Ukraine) to Baghdad (Iraq)

- The sub-region R20 will have the capitals in Kiev (Ukraine) and Kigali (Rwanda) - assistance from Ottawa (Canada).
- The sub-region R21 will have the capitals in Ankara (Turkey) and Khartoum (Sudan) - assistance from Salzburg (Austria).
- The sub-region R22 will have the capitals in Lilongwe (Malawi) and Nicosia (Cyprus) - assistance from Dallas (TX, USA).
- The sub-region R23 will have the capitals in Jerusalem (Israel) and Dodoma (Tanzania) - assistance from Strasbourg (France).
- The sub-region R24 will have the capitals in Damascus (Syria) and Nairobi (Kenya) - assistance from Stuttgart (Germany).
- The sub-region R25 will have the capitals in Krasnodar (Russia) and Addis Ababa (Ethiopia) - assistance from Marseille (France).
- The sub-region R26 will have the capitals in Rostov-on-Don (Russia) and Asmara (Eritrea) - assistance from Leipzig (Germany).
- The sub-region R27 will have the capitals in Stavropol (Russia) and Djibouti (Djibouti) - assistance from Zürich (Switzerland).
- The sub-region R28 will have the capitals in Mosul (Iraq) and Moroni (Comoros) - assistance from Linz (Austria).
- The sub-region R29 will have the capitals in Yerevan (Armenia) and Baghdad (Iraq) - assistance from Göttingen (Germany).

SUN: Nice to see Göttingen (Germany) helping Yerevan (Armenia) and Baghdad (Iraq), in the remarkable sub-region R29.

EARTH: This is the beauty – people from different parts of the world will help each other to get better together.

USA, New York: W 42nd Street, near 8th Avenue, with the Chrysler Building (1930, 320 m, 77 floors, center-right far back).

UK, London: On James Street at Long Acre, City of Westminster, Covent Garden Station, 100 m west of the Royal Opera House.

In Region R3: from Riyadh (Saudi Arabia) to Malé (Maldives)

- The sub-region R30 will have the capitals in Riyadh (Saudi Arabia) and Mogadishu (Somalia) - assistance from Bonn (Germany).
- The sub-region R31 will have the capitals in Baku (Azerbaijan) and Antananarivo (Madagascar) - assistance from Le Mans (France).
- The sub-region R32 will have the capitals in Oral (Kazakhstan) and Tehran (Iran) - assistance from Pisa (Italy).
- The sub-region R33 will have the capitals in Ashgabat (Turkmenistan) and Abu Dhabi (United Arab Emirates) - assistance from Wolfsburg (Germany).
- The sub-region R34 will have the capitals in Magnitogorsk (Russia) and Muscat (Oman) - assistance from Toulouse (France).
- The sub-region R35 will have the capitals in Chelyabinsk (Russia) and Herat (Afghanistan) - assistance from Basel (Switzerland).
- The sub-region R36 will have the capitals in Tyumen (Russia) and Kandahar (Afghanistan) - assistance from Nagoya (Japan).
- The sub-region R37 will have the capitals in Dushanbe (Tajikistan) and Labytnangi (Russia) - assistance from Limoges (France).
- The sub-region R38 will have the capitals in Tashkent (Uzbekistan) and Kabul (Afghanistan) - assistance from Rostock (Germany).
- The sub-region R39 will have the capitals in Islamabad (Pakistan) and Malé (Maldives) - assistance from La Rochelle (France).

SUN: Noteworthy - Pisa (Italy) will be working with Oral (Kazakhstan) and Tehran (Iran) in the stunning sub-region R32.

EARTH: Bringing together different civilizations will be very productive for all people.

SUN: The sub-region R38 will have the capitals in Kabul (Afghanistan) and?

EARTH: Tashkent (Uzbekistan) – it was a typo in a previous edition of the Constitution – we apologize. Nice to see Rostock (Germany) working together with Tashkent (Uzbekistan) and Kabul (Afghanistan) – a really nice combination of cities.

Japan, 13 km north-east from Mount Fuji, the easternmost and largest of the five lakes, Lake Yamanaka is also the third highest lake in Japan, standing at 980 meters above sea level.

In Region R4: from Bishkek (Kyrgyzstan) to Brahmapur (India)

- The sub-region R40 will have the capitals in Bishkek (Kyrgyzstan) and Jaipur (India) - assistance from Osaka (Japan).
- The sub-region R41 will have the capitals in Akola (India) and Kashgar (China) - assistance from Genoa (Italy).
- The sub-region R42 will have the capitals in Almaty (Kazakhstan) and Coimbatore (India) - assistance from Perth (Australia).
- The sub-region R43 will have the capitals in Kuybyshev (Russia) and Agra (India) - assistance from Fukuoka (Japan).
- The sub-region R44 will have the capitals in Vertikos (Russia) and Nagpur (India) - assistance from Coral Bay (Australia).
- The sub-region R45 will have the capitals in Chennai (India) and Colombo (Sri Lanka) - assistance from Sapporo (Japan).
- The sub-region R46 will have the capitals in Lucknow (India) and Fedosikha (Russia) - assistance from Niigata (Japan).
- The sub-region R47 will have the capitals in Bilaspur (India) and Kolpashevo (Russia) - assistance from Albany (Australia).
- The sub-region R48 will have the capitals in Visakhapatnam (India) and Barnaul (Russia) - assistance from Hiroshima (Japan).
- The sub-region R49 will have the capitals in Brahmapur (India) and Tomsk (Russia) - assistance from Yokohama (Japan).

SUN: What a nice combination - Hiroshima (Japan) working with Visakhapatnam (India) and Barnaul (Russia), in the attractive sub-region R48.

EARTH: Yes, people with different experiences working together for a better future for all.
Churchill said it right: If we open a quarrel between past and present, we shall find that we have lost the future.

UK, London: From the British Museum (1753), looking northwest to a nice building after Great Russell Street.

USA, New York: On W 42nd St, the northeast façade of the New York Public Library (1902).

In Region R5: from Kathmandu (Nepal) to Dehong (China)

- The sub-region R50 will have the capitals in Kathmandu (Nepal) and Patna (India) - assistance from Kobe (Japan).
- The sub-region R51 will have the capitals in Bayingol (China) and Novokuznetsk (Russia) - assistance from Vichy (France).
- The sub-region R52 will have the capitals in Thimphu (Bhutan) and Dhaka (Bangladesh) - assistance from Jena (Germany).
- The sub-region R53 will have the capitals in Lhasa (China) and Achinsk (Russia) - assistance from Reims (France).
- The sub-region R54 will have the capitals in Abakan (Russia) and Kumul (China) - assistance from Fribourg (Switzerland).
- The sub-region R55 will have the capitals in Kyzyl (Russia) and Dibrugarh (India) - assistance from Denmark (Australia).
- The sub-region R56 will have the capitals in Bassein (Myanmar) and Tinsukia (India) - assistance from Chiba (Japan).
- The sub-region R57 will have the capitals in Yushu City (China) and Tinskoy (Russia) - assistance from Klagenfurt (Austria).
- The sub-region R58 will have the capitals in Jiuquan (China) and Medan (Indonesia) - assistance from Lucerne (Switzerland).
- The sub-region R59 will have the capitals in Chiang Mai (Thailand) and Dehong (China) - assistance from Mulhouse (France).

SUN: Look at this - Lucerne (Switzerland) working with Jiuquan (China) and Medan (Indonesia) in the astonishing sub-region R58.

EARTH: It is impressive indeed – they will certainly produce great results for everybody.

UK, London: At 31 Endell Street, Covent Garden, The Cross Keys pub, 300 m northwest from the Royal Opera House.

USA, New York: On W 42nd St at Avenue of the Americas, looking northwest at the Bryant Park (left), Grace building (right), Bank of America (next).

In Region R6: from Bangkok (Thailand) to Chita (Russia)

- The sub-region R60 will have the capitals in Bangkok (Thailand) and Kuala Lumpur (Malaysia) - assistance from Besançon (France).
- The sub-region R61 will have the capitals in Vientiane (Laos) and Singapore – assistance from Freiburg im Breisgau (Germany).
- The sub-region R62 will have the capitals in Phnom Penh (Cambodia) and Irkutsk (Russia) – assistance from Baden (Switzerland).
- The sub-region R63 will have the capitals in Palembang (Indonesia), Hanoi (Vietnam) – assistance from Thun (Switzerland).
- The sub-region R64 will have the capitals in Ulan Bator (Mongolia) and Ulan-Ude (Russia) – assistance from Chaumont (France).
- The sub-region R65 will have the capitals in Cirebon (Indonesia) and Nanning (China) – assistance from Vaduz (Lichtenstein).
- The sub-region R66 will have the capitals in Pontianak (Indonesia) and Baotou (China) – assistance from Lugano (Switzerland).
- The sub-region R67 will have the capitals in Surakarta (Indonesia) and Yichang (China) – assistance from Thonon-les-Bain (France).
- The sub-region R68 will have the capitals in Surabaya (Indonesia) and Changsha (China) – assistance from Burgdorf (Switzerland).
- The sub-region R69 will have the capitals in Chita (Russia) and Hong Kong (China) – assistance from Colmar (France).

SUN: Look at Besançon (France) working with Bangkok (Thailand) and Kuala Lumpur (Malaysia), in the lovely sub-region R60.

EARTH: Yes, I'm glad to see them together, improving everybody's life.

SUN: Vita non est vivere, sed valere vita est.

EARTH: Life is not being alive, but being well.

From a bus on Oxford Street at South Molton St (right), looking east to Tissot store, and many other stores.

USA, New York: At 401 Fifth Ave at E 37th St, looking south, TD Bank in a classic nice building.

In Region R7: from Nanchang (China) to Melbourne (Australia)

- The sub-region R70 will have the capitals in Bandar Seri Begawan (Brunei Darussalam) and Nanchang (China) – assistance from Turku (Finland).
- The sub-region R71 will have the capitals in Krasnokamensk (Russia) and Jinan (China) – assistance from St. Gallen (Switzerland).
- The sub-region R72 will have the capitals in Baguio City (Philippines) and Hangzhou (China) – assistance from Dole (France).
- The sub-region R73 will have the capitals in Manila (Philippines) and Taipei (Taiwan, China) – assistance from Metz (France).
- The sub-region R74 will have the capitals in Kupang (Indonesia) and Shanghai (China) – assistance from Davos (Switzerland).
- The sub-region R75 will have the capitals in Pyongyang (North Korea) and Seoul (South Korea) – assistance from Versailles (France).
- The sub-region R76 will have the capitals in Vladivostok (Russia) and Busan (South Korea) – assistance from Innsbruck (Austria).
- The sub-region R77 will have the capitals in Kyoto (Japan) and Khabarovsk (Russia) – assistance from Germering (Germany).
- The sub-region R78 will have the capitals in Nagoya (Japan) and Komsomolsk-on-Amur (Russia) – assistance from Venice (Italy).
- The sub-region R79 will have the capitals in Sendai (Japan) and Melbourne (Australia) – assistance from St. Moritz (Switzerland).

SUN: One cannot have a better combination than this - Versailles (France) working with Pyongyang (North Korea) and Seoul (South Korea) in the marvelous sub-region R75, for the benefit of all people.

EARTH: Yes, it will be a great success.
Confucius helps us: Success depends upon previous preparation.

Finland, Helsinki Central railway station (1907 – 1914), on Brunnsgatan, in the city center.

UK, London: Wellington (1769-1852) Arch (1830, four-horse chariot 1912), at southeast corner of Hyde Park, and western corner of Green Park

In Region R8: from Anchorage (Alaska, USA) to Lima (Peru)

- The sub-region R80 will have the capitals in Uelen (Russia) and Anchorage (Alaska, USA), – assistance from Zug (Switzerland).
- The sub-region R81 will have the capitals in Vancouver (Canada) and San Jose (CA, USA) – assistance from Odense (Denmark).
- The sub-region R82 will have the capitals in Vernon (Canada) and Los Angeles (CA, USA) – assistance from Amstetten (Austria).
- The sub-region R83 will have the capitals in Calgary (Canada) and Tijuana (Mexico) – assistance from Chur (Switzerland).
- The sub-region R84 will have the capitals in Hermosillo (Mexico) and Tucson (AR, USA) – assistance from Bergen (Norway).
- The sub-region R85 will have the capitals in Chihuahua (Mexico) and Regina (Canada) – assistance from Gothenburg (Sweden).
- The sub-region R86 will have the capitals in San Luis Potosi City (Mexico) and Winnipeg (Canada) – assistance from Yverdon-les-Bains (Switzerland).
- The sub-region R87 will have the capitals in Tulsa (OK, USA) and Veracruz (Mexico) – assistance from Bregenz (Austria).
- The sub-region R88 will have the capitals in Memphis (TN, USA) and San José (Costa Rica) – assistance from Uppsala (Sweden).
- The sub-region R89 will have the capitals in Lima (Peru) and Boston (MA, USA) – assistance from Tampere (Finland).

SUN: Now another wonderful combination - Zug (Switzerland) working with Uelen (Russia) and Anchorage (Alaska, USA), in the attractive sub-region R80.

EARTH: One can expect really astonishing results, good for all people.
Here it is good to remember Jefferson: "All tyranny needs to gain a foothold is for people of good conscience to remain silent."

USA, Boston (founded in 1630): tall ships from many countries, at the Boston Fish Pier (opened in 1915).

Rome. North-west view of Rome from Altare della Patria (1925), with Via del Teatro di Marcello (13 AD, down left), and Basilica Papale di San Pietro in Vaticano (1506, center back).

In Region R9: from La Paz (Bolivia) to London (United Kingdom)

- The sub-region R90 will have the capitals in La Paz (Bolivia) and Bangor (Maine, USA) – assistance from Aosta (Italy).
- The sub-region R91 will have the capitals in Caracas (Venezuela) and Road Town (British Virgin Islands) – assistance from Obergoms (Switzerland).
- The sub-region R92 will have the capitals in Buenos Aires (Argentina) and Fort-de-France (Martinique) – assistance from Freudenstadt (Germany).
- The sub-region R93 will have the capitals in Asuncion (Paraguay) and Montevideo (Uruguay) – assistance from Winterthur (Switzerland).
- The sub-region R94 will have the capitals in Cayenne (French Guiana), St. John's (Canada) – assistance from Novara (Italy).
- The sub-region R95 will have the capitals in Rio de Janeiro (Brazil) and Dakar (Senegal) – assistance from Toyama (Japan).
- The sub-region R96 will have the capitals in Freetown (Sierra Leone) and Lisbon (Portugal) – assistance from Kawasaki (Japan).
- The sub-region R97 will have the capitals in Bamako (Mali) and Athlone (Ireland) – assistance from Ulm (Germany).
- The sub-region R98 will have the capitals in Yamoussoukro (Cote d'Ivoire) and Madrid (Spain) – assistance from Okayama (Japan).
- The sub-region R99 will have the capitals in Ouagadougou (Burkina Faso) and London (United Kingdom) - assistance from Vaasa (Finland).

SUN: Breath taking - Toyama (Japan) working with Rio de Janeiro (Brazil) and Dakar (Senegal), in the stupendous sub-region R95.

EARTH: I cannot find words – they will certainly significantly contribute to the success of this Constitution of the World! Between Toyama and Rio de Janeiro there are over 18,000 km, and between Rio de Janeiro (Brazil) and Dakar (Senegal), over 5,000 km, and with video and phone contacts, the collaboration will work fine.

Finland, Helsinki: a Baltic Sea canal from west to east, near Ruoholahdenpuisto, seen from a bridge on Bottenhavsgatan, near Helsinki Conservatory of Music (left).

UK, London: From a bus going southwest on Pall Mall, Royal Opera Arcade Gallery (center, hosting art exhibitions and events).

5.4. Level 3 Management: Ten L3 friendly managers

Ten L3 friendly managers for the 10 regions, who will supervise and assist the 10 L2 managers of the 10 sub-regions of each region, for a total of about 770,000,000 people for each region.

SUN: These 10 regions, each with about 770 M people, are really big.

EARTH: Yes, only two countries now are bigger, therefore they will require effective and energetic management.

- The Region R0 will have the first capitals in Bern (Switzerland) and Libreville (Gabon) – assistance from Oxford (UK). For better quality and consistency of the management, we'll have the first two cities from the region R0, and the third city from outside. Actually, being inside the same country Terra, any city, sub-region or region can ask for advice or help from anybody.

- The Region R1 will have the first capitals in Warsaw (Poland) and Pretoria (South Africa) – assistance from Miami (FL, USA).

- The Region R2 will have the first capitals in Moscow (Russia) and Cairo (Egypt) – assistance from Grenoble (France).

- The Region R3 will have the first capitals in Astana (Kazakhstan) and Karachi (Pakistan), – assistance from Montpellier (France).

- The Region R4 will have the first capitals in New Delhi (India) and Novosibirsk (Russia) – assistance from Magdeburg (Germany).

- The Region R5 will have the first capitals in Krasnoyarsk (Russia) and Urumqi (China) – assistance from Avignon (France).

- The Region R6 will have the first capitals in Jakarta (Indonesia) and Beijing (China) – assistance from Neuchâtel (Switzerland).

- The Region R7 will have the first capitals in Tokyo (Japan) and Sydney (Australia) – assistance from Malmö (Sweden).

- The Region R8 will have the first capitals in Washington (USA) and Mexico City (Mexico) – assistance from Bellinzona (Switzerland).

- The Region R9 will have the first capitals in Halifax (Canada) and Brasilia (Brazil) – assistance from Biel (Switzerland).

Japan, Tokyo, Shinjuku: suspended streets between tall buildings.

SUN: Really global - Malmö (Sweden) working with Tokyo (Japan) and Sydney (Australia) in the inspiring region R7.

EARTH: They will enhance the beauty of the world. Malmö (Sweden) to Tokyo (Japan) is over 8,500 km, and Tokyo (Japan) to Sydney (Australia) is over 7,700 km.

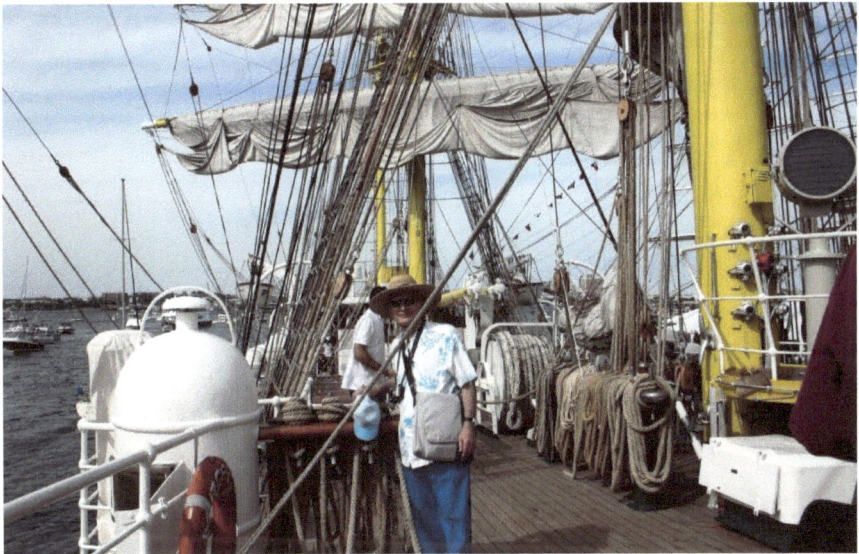

USA, Boston (founded in 1630): on a visiting tall ship, at the Boston Fish Pier (opened in 1915).

5.5. Level 4 Management: very friendly 10 Advisers

5.5.1 - L4 very friendly 10 Advisers of the world, who will supervise and assist the 10 L3 managers of the 10 regions of the Earth, for a total of about 7,700,000,000 people – all the people on Earth, citizens of Peaceful Terra.

SUN: Now we are at the top level – great responsibility.

EARTH: Indeed, the 10 Advisers will calmly and intelligently manage the world, for the benefit of the people on the planet.
Here Goethe helps: All intelligent thoughts have already been thought; what is necessary is only to try to think them again.

Japan, Mount Fuji (Fuji-san, 3776 m), seen from Minamitsuru District, circa 15 km north-est from Mount Fuji.

5.5.2 - The L4 very friendly 10 Advisers of the world will be located each in one the ten Regions R0, R1,…, R9. For example, in the beginning, for the first month (then changing every month), the ten Advisers of the world will be located:

- in R0: Barcelona (Spain)
- in R1: Benghazi (Libya)
- in R2: Addis Ababa (Ethiopia)
- in R3: Hyderabad (Pakistan)
- in R4: Bhopal (India)
- in R5: Mandalay (Myanmar)
- in R6: Nanchong (China)
- in R7: Khabarovsk (Russia)
- in R8: Houston (USA)
- in R9: Recife (Brazil)

Finland, Helsinki: a commercial harbor in the south-west of the city, near Hietalahdenranta, with the boat Aranda.SUN: Good locations for beginning.

EARTH: Yes, and they will change the location every month, to be close to as many people as possible – this mobility will help them understand what the people want, and how to achieve the people's objectives fast and efficient.

5.5.3 – These ten L4 Advisers will be in permanent contact with each other, and with the L3 Advisers, for the best management of the world.

5.5.4 – The ten L4 Advisers will work by consensus only.

SUN: Very important management rule.

EARTH: Yes, the 10 Advisors must be talented enough to be able to negotiate fast any disagreements between them, and quickly arrive at the best common decision for the benefit of all people.

5.5.5 - The ten L4 Advisers will be elected from the 10 regions, and each of them will be the First Adviser (*First among equals* – from Latin: Primus inter pares) for one month, by rotation.

5.5.6 - The First Adviser only coordinates the work of the other 9 Advisors for one month.

SUN: No question that these management rules will create the necessary harmony for the world.

EARTH: Yes, the 10 Advisers represent the world, they were elected to improve the world, therefore they must harmoniously work together for the benefit of all people.

UK, London: On Pall Mall East SW, the Wellington building (center), Strand Palace Hotel (center left), building on right built in 1834.

5.5.7 – The ten L4 Advisers will move each month from a first capital of a region to the second capital of another region, at random (or based on urgency, if an emergency occurred). This mobility is essential for having a long period of tranquility and harmony.

SUN: Very good mobility.

EARTH: Yes, the 10 Advisers were elected from their regions, but they must stay in all the regions, to understand the local problems of all the regions, in order to make decisions which will benefit all the people.

5.5.8 - The First Adviser, on the last day of each month, will present in writing for the world (no more than 5 standard pages) a clear and precise Monthly World Report, with a list of finished and unfinished tasks.

SUN: This is essential.

EARTH: Indeed, a clear and precise Monthly World Report (5 pages), with a list of finished and unfinished tasks, will help everybody understand what was done, what remains to be done, and what ideas are about doing them fast and correct.

5.5.9 - The other 9 Advisers will add their comments to the Monthly World Report (no more than half a page each - total report less than 9.5 pages).

SUN: Comments are always welcome.

EARTH: Harmonious comments, which want to help, give new ideas, etc.

Finland, Helsinki: a government building on Abrahaminkatu, north-east of a large square

5.5.10 - The top 10 Advisers will manage Police and all other Departments.

SUN: Important to put Police first.

EARTH: Yes, Police is the only Department which can use some force, in extreme situations, therefore there is need to have strict control on how to use this force, and actually to try to minimize the use of force, and maximize the use of calm dialog, medical assistance, and friendly approach.

5.5.11 - For obvious uncooperative or improper attitude of one top Advisor X, the other 9 can replace X with X's number 2, and X will receive appropriate medical treatment.

5.5.12 - When vacancies happen for Advisors, the number 2 for those Advisors will fill the vacancies.

5.5.13 - All the activities of all Advisors will be recorded in computers and videos, and on paper, for people to be able to see what they are doing.

5.5.14 - Advisors at all levels should work 40 hours/week, with 4 weeks of vacation, but many services (medical, police (firemen should be part of the police), emergency, volunteers) should be non-stop.

5.5.15 – Advisors' compensation should be the world annual average salary (in 2019 less than $10,000) plus 4% of that world average salary, for level 4 (total $10,400), + 3 % for level 3, and so on. They all should work to increase the world average salary, in order to get themselves an increase.

5.5.16 - All the other world government employees will have a compensation close to the average compensation of the people in the area where they are located.

5.5.17 - All Advisors are free to speak about their administrative work, with modesty.

SUN: This modesty is so important.

EARTH: Sure, all Advisors work for people, and only the people will have a say about Advisers' administrative work.

5.5.18 - All spending proposals from Advisers must be approved by their 5 assistants (doctors, mathematicians, CEOs, engineers and teachers), and must have an already existing funding in the budget.

SUN: These spending proposals are always problematic.

EARTH: For this reason, they must be approved by all assistants (doctors, mathematicians, CEOs, engineers and teachers), and must have an already existing funding in the budget.

Rome: Center: Columna Traiani (113 AD) with a band (180 m) of carved reliefs. Left: Altare della Patria (1925).

5.5.19 - Advisors (and all the others) cannot declare war, reprisals or capture land or water.

5.5.20 - Advisors (and all the others) cannot raise and support armies, navy, or any military forces.

SUN: These statements are really fundamental.

EARTH: Indeed, all the people want peace, freedom and prosperity, therefore it is natural to have these very clear, simple and fundamental requirements.
And we remember Hoover: Older men declare war. But it is youth that must fight and die.

5.5.21 - At least 7 of the top 10 Advisers should be present every working day.

5.5.22 - The Advisors will be located in the current government buildings, and the excess government buildings and properties will be sold, in order to increase the budget, and to reduce the expenses.

SUN: Normal requirements.

EARTH: Yes, the government should frugal, simple and modest.
Jefferson, as always, helps: "A wise and frugal Government, which shall restrain men from injuring one another, which shall leave them otherwise free to regulate their own pursuits of industry and improvement, and shall not take from the mouth of labor the bread it has earned. This is the sum of good government."

Washington (1790), National Archives and Records Administration building (1935), on Constitution Avenue.

USA, New York: On 5th Ave (right), Broadway (next left), at E 23rd St by the Flatiron (Fuller) Building (1902, 87 m, center right triangular 22-story steel-framed tower, E 22nd St behind), Madison Square Park (left).

5.5.23 - In order to better know the world government, to help it, and, especially, to improve it, all able people of the world will work as volunteers at least one day per year in each of the seven departments.

SUN: Excellent idea!

EARTH: Indeed, this brings the government close to the people, which pay all their salaries and expenses – a close cooperation between people and their friendly government is a necessity for a harmonious world.
Good to remember Anatole France: "If a million people say a foolish thing, it is still a foolish thing."

5.5.24 - After each Monthly World Report, a public opinion survey about the report should be taken, and presented to all Advisors.

SUN: Clearly useful.

EARTH: Sure, people must express their opinions on the work of their Advisors, and Advisors must keep in mind that they have to work hard and smart to fulfill their obligations for all people.
Cicero comes handily: "Nature has planted in our minds an insatiable longing to see the truth."

Japan, 13 km north-east from Mount Fuji, the easternmost and largest of the five lakes, Lake Yamanaka is also the third highest lake in Japan, standing at 980 meters above sea level.

France, Paris: Jardin du Carrousel and Pavillion de Marsan, at the west end of the north part of Musée du Louvre; it also was located at the northern end of Palais des Tuileries (1564 – 1883 demolished).

5.5.25 - All activities of the Advisors, and others from the small World Government, will be available to the people on a website.

5.5.26 - The top 10 Advisers (and all the others) will collaborate via e-mail, telephone, videoconferences, mail, or face to face, when needed, to produce practical results for all people, very fast.

SUN: Bottom line - produce practical results for all people, very fast.

EARTH: This is it – no words, just produce practical results for all people, very fast.

SUN: Facta non verba.

EARTH: Deeds, not words.

USA, New York: On Fifth Avenue at E 40th St, looking southwest at Mid-Manhattan Library, a New York Public Library (1895, 1908, 87 branches (Carnegie libraries (Andrew Carnegie (1835-1919)))), 53 millions of books and other items, the 2nd largest public library in the United States (behind the Library of Congress), and the fourth largest in the world (after British Library (170 M), Library of Congress (160 M), and Library and Archives Canada (54 M)) image archive (left), having thousands of photos, posters, illustrations, and other images.

5.6. Five Assistants

5.6.1 - Each Advisor, and each manager at all levels, will have 5 immediate assistants:
1) a mathematician for finance and all other calculations,
2) a medical doctor for keeping everybody healthy, calm, polite, friendly and optimist,
3) a CEO for good management,
4) an engineer for all practical projects, and
5) a teacher for education, training and related areas.

SUN: Well, this is the real hope.

EARTH: Certainly, only by having highly knowledgeable and talented people, it will be possible to implement the many complex and pressing tasks, which are in the front of the World Government.

SUN: Dum spiro, spero.

EARTH: While I breathe, I hope.

5.6.2 – The five assistants play a key role, because they are highly qualified professionals, who actually will carry on the practical management of the world.

5.6.3 - The five assistants' integrity, professionalism and friendliness will significantly improve the quality of the world and local governments.

5.6.4 - The five assistants are really the experts. They will assist the Advisors and all levels of management, in order to have an efficient, correct and professional working of the world government at all levels.

SUN: Clear statements.

EARTH: Yes, they give real hope that the world government will work how the people expect.

SUN: Aut disce aut discede.

EARTH: Either learn or leave.

USA, New York: On Fifth Ave at East 34th St, the Graduate Center of the City Univ. of New York (left), a small building across Empire State Building.

5.7. The Honorific World Observer

5.7.1 - A Honorific World Observer will be quietly elected by direct vote – starting, for example, 1st September 2022 - for only one 3 years term, with the main duty to observe that the top 10 Advisers efficiently perform their duties, and keep their words – if they don't, they will be changed.

SUN: Now comes the Honorific World Observer.

EARTH: Yes, this Observer is needed to observe and assist the 10 Advisors – they all must efficiently perform their duties, and keep their words.

5.7.2 - For managers and for everybody else, keeping their word is a serious and strict requirement.

5.7.3 - The Honorific World Observer has this responsibility for the top 10 Advisors, but all people will pay attention to this. Words must become again important and respected.

SUN: Finally, the words will count again.

EARTH: Sure, it is strict necessary to have the words again important and respected.

Finland, Helsinki: beautiful buildings on Mikonkatu, close to Aleksanterinkatu, 200 m south-east of the Helsinki Central Railway Station.

5.8. Small World Government with 7 Departments

5.8.1 - All the employees of the World Government are temporary, and must reapply for their positions every year.

5.8.2 – There is no need for unions.

5.8.3 - The World Government will be limited to:
1) the Office of the Honorific Observer (less than 10 employees),
2) the Office of the top ten Advisors (less than 100 employees), and
3) 7 small departments.

SUN: Clear and useful statements.

EARTH: Yes, the World Government works for all people, and should have clear limitations, not to waste people's money and time.

5.8.4 - The World Government will have these 7 small departments:

SUN: 7 is a good number.

EARTH: Yes, not too small, and, especially, not too big.

- Tax Department

- Collects taxes of 15% of the income of people and revenue of companies.

- The Manager of the Tax Department is appointed for a three-year term by the World 10 Advisers.

- The number of employees must be under 50,000, with excellent computers, and advanced software.

SUN: Good beginning.

EARTH: Yes, the Tax Department is important, brings revenue to the World Government, and the government must use this money for people's benefit.

Rome. Isola Tiberina (left), Pons Cestius (27 BC, right up), viewed from Ponte Garibaldi, 1888, joining Regola & Trastevere (right).

Rome. Down: a part of Forum Augustum (2 BC). Back: a part of Forum Traiani (113 AD), including Columna Traiani (113, center back), with a band (180 m) of carved reliefs, which winds around the Trajan's Column, describing Trajan's Dacian war campaigns (101-102 and 105-106 AD). After Trajan's death, his 6 m statue was on top until 1587. His ashes and later those of his wife Plotina were placed in the base of the column.

- Treasury

Treasury will control all the financial issues, including:
- antitrust
- fiscal service
- financial cooperation
- financing bank
- world reserve system
- world budget using only revenue, no borrowing, and spending only on strict necessary needs
– all the budgets, at all levels, will have a 2% surplus, which will be returned to the taxpayers
- register of all government papers and activities
- archives and records
- assist all people to have savings accounts for old age (the old age will be starting around 70), and 10% of their income should automatically go to their savings accounts. For those unable to work, their doctors and mathematicians will decide case by case.
- bankruptcies, in general, will be discouraged, and when strict necessary, will be analyzed and solved, case by case, by the doctors, mathematicians and CEOs who worked with the people who asked the bankruptcy.
- encourage all families to assist their parents, grandparents, and great-grandparents.
- housing finance
- housing for all people
- no homelessness
- consumer financial protection
- pensions
- privacy
- current social security until replaced by personal savings
- personnel management
- general services for the world government
- each the 10 regions will receive 2.5% of the world taxes - at least 30% of the money will be sent to villages and cities.
- each of the 100 sub-regions will receive 0.25% of the world taxes. At least 40% of the money will be sent to villages and cities.

- The World Central Bank will include all current central banks – starting, for example, on May 1st, 2023.
- The Special Credit Card (SCC) will be issued by the World Central Bank.
- Advisors will create a new world currency, named, for example, "coin", and all the other currencies will be exchanged for coins. The World Central Bank will implement the details.
- The counterfeiting and all other bad things, which some sick people do, will be medically treated (in specialized medical institutions when necessary), and those who did bad things will pay all the expenses, and will reimburse the victims. Victims will always be very protected, and helped to recover the losses from the attackers.

SUN: There are many relevant responsibilities in this Treasury Department.

EARTH: Yes, like:
- world reserve system
- world budget using only revenue, no borrowing, and spending only on strict necessary needs
– all the budgets, at all levels, will have a 2% surplus, which will be returned to the taxpayers
- assist all people to have savings accounts for old age
- housing for all people
- The World Central Bank will include all current central banks
- The Special Credit Card (SCC) will be issued by the World Central Bank.
- Advisors will create a new world currency, named, for example, "coin", and all the other currencies will be exchanged for coins. The World Central Bank will implement the details.

UK, London: On Broad Ct looking northeast, off Bow Street to the northeast, 50 m north of the Royal Opera House at Covent Garden (1732, 1808, 1858, 1999, capacity 2,256; in 1734, Covent Garden presented its first ballet, Pygmalion), the bronze statue Young Dancer, by the Italian-born (in Mestre, near Venice, in 1921) British sculptor Enzo Plazzotta (1921-1981 (age 60)). To the right up, five red telephone boxes, at 5 Broad Ct, a tourist attraction.

- People Assistance Department

It will assist people in general, including:
- parent assistance
- dispute resolution
- in very simple disputes or culpa levis (ordinary negligence, like late payments, etc.), one single assistant will decide within minutes, and all people will go back to work
- census every 5 years
- election assistance every 20 months
 - special credit cards
- people protection against abuses from anybody
- completely eliminate corruption, organized crime and drug trafficking
- all people in the world will remain in their places, and the improvements will come to them. Those who want to move to other places, will need first a special invitation from at least 10 people (not family related) where they want to move.
- all the Tribunals and related areas will be transformed in people assistance services, based on friendliness, collaboration and goodwill.
- It is well understood that no excessive bail will be required, no excessive fines imposed, no cruel and unusual punishments applied, but, at the same time, it is well understood that a person who did a bad thing will receive the necessary corrective medical treatment, and will reimburse all people who suffered damages, and the medical treatment. The victims will always receive special attention.
- Nobility (King, Prince, etc.) could continue to exist in some places, but they should not interfere with activities of the Advisors, and actually should help them.
- food safety
- trash & recycling
- free commerce
- jobs assistance
- postal service
- labor safety and harmonious relations
- land, water

- volunteers
- fitness, sport, tourism
- 10 world holidays: the normal 4 Earth events (2 solstices (around 21 June, around 21 December), and 2 equinoxes (around 21 March, around 21 September), Mother's Day on 1st May, Father's Day on 6 August, Children's Day on 6 November, Grandparents' Day on 6 February, and 2 optional days (like Thanksgiving or a Religious Day (Christmas), and New Year).

SUN: This new People Assistance Department is a real joy!

EARTH: Yes, it has plenty of very useful responsibilities:
- parent assistance
- dispute resolution
- census every 5 years
- election assistance every 20 months
- special credit cards
- people protection against abuses from anybody
- completely eliminate corruption, organized crime and drug trafficking
- all people in the world will remain in their places, and the improvements will come to them
- food safety
- trash & recycling
- free commerce
- jobs assistance
- postal service
- labor safety and harmonious relations

SUN: Cicero helps here:

EARTH: Never go to excess, but let moderation be your guide. Faithfulness and truth are the most sacred excellences and endowments of the human mind.

- Medical Department

It will manage all medical and healthcare related areas, including:
- human services
- conflict resolution
- families, children, elderly
- medicine approval
- disease control and prevention
- medical doctors and assistants will make regular home visits, at least once a year, to all people, to keep them healthy, and to prevent illnesses.
- medical research: cancer, heart, lung, blood, arthritis, surgical robotics, connected computers for healthcare, etc.
- healthy homes, streets, stores, working places, etc.
- healthy aging
- all misunderstandings, disagreements or conflicts of any nature will be treated by medical personnel (with police help when strict necessary), until all is back to normal.
- no prisons are necessary, only specialized medical institutions (in simple cases, the places where the treated people live can be used, with the necessary limitations and surveillance)
- If a person X is considered that did a bad thing, X will have, within 3 days, a discussion with one or more doctors and other assistants, and will be informed of the nature and cause of the bad thing; including witnesses against and for him. Then a decision will be taken within other 3 days, by a group of doctors and other assistants. Victims of bad people will always have priority to discuss their problems with one or more doctors and other assistants, and quick decisions will be taken within 3 days, by a group of doctors and other assistants. Protection of victims has always priority.
- in order to better know the world government, to help it, and, especially, to improve it, all able people of the world will work as volunteers at least one day per year in the local facility of this department, which will have a special office for managing this volunteer work.

– all people will have government medical insurance, and they can also have private medical insurance
– there will be doctors working for the government 100%, or only part-time, or having only private practice, all with reasonable salaries and fees.
– there will be government pharmaceutical institutions and private pharmaceutical companies, offering reasonable priced medicines, without advertising to the general public.

SUN: The very essential Medical Department is certainly full of responsibilities.

EARTH: Of course:
- human services
- conflict resolution
- families, children, elderly
- medicine approval
- disease control and prevention
- medical doctors and assistants will make regular home visits, at least once a year, to all people
And all the others.

SUN: Terence is here…

EARTH: I am a man, and whatever concerns humanity is of interest to me.

France, Paris: The Institut de France (1795, initially in Louvre, moved in 1805 by Napoléon in this baroque building finished in 1684, for Collège des Quatre-Nations) is a revered French cultural society which includes five académies, the most famous being Académie française (1635) and. Académie des sciences (Academy of Sciences), founded in 1666. The Institute, located on Quai de Conti, manages about 1,000 foundations, as well as museums and châteaux. Its Mazarine Library is France's oldest public library.

- Police

Police will provide assistance for:
- accidents
- disasters
- complete elimination of nuclear, chemical and biological arms, firearms and explosives
- world complete security
- world cooperation
- conflict reduction and resolution
- investigations
- emergency assistance
- training
- delinquency prevention in general, and especially juvenile
- protection of Advisors, important government buildings, etc.
- extended surveillance and reconnaissance to prevent bad events
- fire protection
- volunteers to help police
- police will be present at public meetings, services, shows, etc., in order to protect the public
- public order
- ensuring traffic safety
- completely eliminate corruption, organized crime and drug trafficking
- movement of people based on civilized rules
- assist and protect those who have encountered violence
- World Police and specialists from the former United Nations and Interpol will be ready and very mobile for urgent and special operations, when they are needed.
- Police will be the only department which will have some small arms, in order to stop some very bad people (who are very sick).
- a small manufacturing and maintenance of arms unit will be part of the Police Department, under strict control.
- Police will work with medical personnel, mathematicians, CEOs, engineers, teachers and others, to make sure that all the people on

the Planet are in good mental health, in order to prevent bad situations. This is also a major responsibility of all Advisors.
- prevention of bad events
- The Advisors will allocate the necessary budget for Police, and Police will assist people in need.

SUN: No question that police is necessary and important.

EARTH: Certainly, and they will become friends of all people, and will help them:
- accidents
- disasters
- complete elimination of nuclear, chemical and biological arms, firearms and explosives
- world complete security
- world cooperation
- conflict reduction and resolution
- investigations
- emergency assistance

SUN: And here comes Churchill...

EARTH: If you go on with this nuclear arms race, all you are going to do is make the rubble bounce.

UK, London: From Charing Cross Rd, looking southeast to the northwest part of the front part of the English Anglican church St Martin in the Fields (1724, at the northeast corner of Trafalgar Square in the City of Westminster, spire height 59 m, 12 bells, tenor bell weight 1,486 kg, excavations under found a grave from about 410 AD (Roman era), in 1222 there was a church here, in 1542 Henry VIII rebuilt the church, in 1606 James I enlarged the church). It is famous for its regular lunchtime and evening concerts; Academy of St Martin-in-the-Fields performs here, and many other ensembles.

- Education Department

- Over 2 billions of children in the world will get a solid peace-oriented education, to give a solid peace-oriented foundation for a good, free, peaceful and prosperous life.
- Education is very important – teachers will work with parents and grandparents, to educate the children to leave healthy in a sustainable peace, liberty and prosperity.
- Discipline must be strict, and those who do not behave properly, will get medical assistance.
- The world will have 4 school levels (SLs) of education:
SL1 – Kindergarten – 2 years: age 5 and 6
SL2 – Primary School – 4 years: age 7, 8, 9 and 10
SL3 – Secondary School – 3 years: age 11, 12 and 13
SL4 – High School or Vocational School – 4 years: age 14, 15, 16 and 17
- A World Library will include the Library of Congress and all the other great libraries – they will remain where they are now, but will be digitally interconnected, and accessible from any place in the world.
- adult education: technical, career
- training for employment
- management training
- post high school education
- peace education
- world constitution education

SUN: Without good education, there is no good future.

EARTH: Exactly so – for this much attention will be given to good education.
- adult education: technical, career
- training for employment

- management training
- post high school education
- peace education
- world constitution education

Aristotle: The roots of education are bitter, but the fruit is sweet.
Plato: Ignorance, the root and stem of all evil.

UK, London: The north and west sides of the church St. Martin-in-the Fields, with Horatio Nelson's (1758-1805) Column (right) in Trafalgar Square.

UK, London: The program by Candlelight at St Martin in the Fields, on Friday, October 14, 2016 at 7:30 PM, with Antonio Vivaldi (1678 in Venice-1741 (age 63) Vienna), Johann Sebastian Bach (1685-1750 (age 65)), Francesco Geminiani (1687-1762 (age 75)), George Frideric Handel (1685 Germany-1759 (age 74) London UK, buried at Westminster Abbey), Wolfgang Amadeus Mozart (1756 Salzburg, Austria-1791 (age 35) Vienna, Austria), Johann Pachelbel (1653 Nuremberg, Germany-1706 (age 53) Nuremberg, Germany).

- Science & Technology Department.

It will help in the areas of:
- mathematics
- statistics
- science
- technology
- Algorithmic Governance will be an essential tool for a better and impartial governing of the world, used by the Advisers elected by people. Mathematicians from all countries will work to improve the Algorithmic Governance, to better serve the people.
- cyberspace complete security will be achieved and strictly maintained
- information systems
- computer services
- Internet
- scientific cooperation
- economic development at the world level
- infrastructure improvement and maintenance at the world level
- innovation and improvements in all areas, at the world level
- transportation at the world level
- safety
- security
- aviation
- highway
- cars
- railroads without noise
- maritime administration
- logistics
- strategic planning at the world level
- public works
- fleet maintenance
- standards: weights, measures, etc.
- research at the world level
- risk analysis
- laboratories

- engineering
- communications at the world level
- telecommunications
- networks
- peaceful nuclear energy use at the world level
- safety
- waste
- electrical power
- oceanic analysis at the world level
- atmospheric analysis at the global level
- meteorological service and prognosis at the global level
- world resources analysis
- sustainable use of world resources
- geographical and geological activity
- product safety at the global level
- hazardous material and chemical safety
- government broadcasting (radio, tv, Internet, newspaper, etc.) including news, scientific and technical information
- private broadcasting will continue, but the world government must be able to directly inform the people, without intermediaries
- space exploration and expansion at the world level – very important for the future
- patent and trademark
- intellectual rights
- all government work, which can be done by private companies, will be contracted with the best and reasonably priced private companies. At the same time, the government should always have competitive services for people – from plumbing and electrical help, to mortgage and buying or selling a house.

SUN: This new department has a large number of heavy tasks.

EARTH: As expected, science and technology are becoming more important every day:
- cyberspace complete security will be achieved and strictly maintained

- information systems
- computer services
- Internet
- scientific cooperation
- economic development at the world level
- infrastructure improvement and maintenance at the world level
- innovation and improvements in all areas, at the world level
- transportation at the world level
- safety
- security
- aviation
- highway
- cars
- railroads without noise
- maritime administration
- logistics
- strategic planning at the world level
- public works

And all the others.

Pasteur: Science knows no country, because knowledge belongs to humanity, and is the torch which illuminates the world.

Galileo Galilei: In questions of science, the authority of a thousand is not worth the humble reasoning of a single individual.

UK, Oxford: From Broad St, looking south to the northeastern side of the Sheldonian Theatre (1669, classical concerts, lectures, ceremonies, capacity 1,000, by Gilbert Sheldon (1598-1677, Archbishop of Canterbury), 3 busts (center line), Bodleian Library (1602, left back, main research library of the University of Oxford, over 12 M items).

Proposition 6. Elections every 20 months

6.1. The Advisers should be elected every 20 months for one term only. If an Adviser X was elected for a term T1, then the next term T2 will have another Advisor Y. For the next term T3, X can be elected again, but the next term T4 will have a new Adviser, and so on. All levels of Advisers (minimum age 25 years) can be elected, not consecutively, at most 4 times (maximum 80 months = 6 years and 8 months).

6.2 All the employees in Government will respect Seneca's (circa 1,960 years ago) aphorism "To govern is to serve, not to rule", and Hippocrates' (over 2,400 years ago) aphorism "Make a habit of two things: to help; or at least to do no harm."

SUN: Excellent ideas.

EARTH: Indeed:
Advisers should be elected every 20 months for one term only.
All levels of Advisers (minimum age 25 years) can be elected, not consecutively, at most 4 times (maximum 80 months = 6 years and 8 months).
To govern is to serve, not to rule.
Make a habit of two things: to help; or at least to do no harm.

6.3 Advisers should have exceptional results obtained from their work, and based on these results, plus modesty, moderation, good character, friendliness, sharp mind, wisdom, good morals, and intense desire to help people, they will be elected, without any campaigning, publicity, fundraising, donations, debates, propaganda, political parties, advertising, or similar activities.

UK, London: A beautiful Lloyds Bank (founded in Birmingham in 1765 by Taylors and Sampson Lloyd (1699-1779, iron manufacturer and banker)) building in London (founded by the Romans, who named it Londinium (a settlement established on the current site of the City of London around AD 43 (by Claudius (10 BC – 54 AD)). Its bridge over the River Thames turned the city into a road nexus and major port, serving as a major commercial center in Roman Britain until its abandonment around 420). London's ancient core, the City of London, largely retains its 2.9 km^2 medieval boundaries.

6.4 There will be use of advanced digital technology, which opens up entirely new opportunities for developing direct elections, and public control of the institutions, improving the transparency of the election procedure, and taking into account the interests and opinions of each voter (over the age of 21, who are not in a special medical institution for bad behavior or for mental health).

SUN: The things are getting better.

EARTH: Sure:
Advisers should have exceptional results obtained from their work.
Use of advanced digital technology.
Thucydides: Ignorance is bold and knowledge reserved.

6.5. An Election Commission of 110 representatives from the 10 regions and from the 100 sub-regions, elected separately for 5 years, will have to examine the qualifications of all the candidates for Advisers, and for other senior management positions. Unqualified candidates will be asked to improve their qualifications, and then to try again later.

SUN: Now this is really necessary.

EARTH: Right, an Election Commission of 110 representatives from the 10 regions and from the 100 sub-regions, will have to examine the qualifications of all the candidates.
Otto von Bismarck: People never lie so much as before an election, during a war, or after a hunt.

UK, London: From the northeast corner of Trafalgar Square, south of the National Gallery, looking southwest to Vice Admiral Horatio Nelson's (1758-1805 (aged 47), buried at St Paul's Cathedral) Column, and the equestrian statue of King George IV (1762-1830 (aged 68), King 1820-1830, patron of architecture, the eldest son of King George III (1738-1820 (aged 81), Reign 1760-1820 (59 years), during his reign, the American colonies created the U. S. A.)).

6.6. It is important to refresh the management, and to bring new people to help the big family of 7.7 B people. The older generations, who performed well, will be retained in important roles, because experience and maturity count very much. At least two months before the retirement, they will kindly be asked to transfer their expertise to the younger generation. Even after retirement, they will occasionally be invited to share their expertise.

6.7. In every election, with every winner, will be other two for number 2 and number 3. The number 2 and number 3 for each management position will be used when number 1 is not available (vacation, sick, etc.). They will constantly work for number 1, helping to solve urgent problems for the people.

6.8. Good elections are essential for the future.

There has been a tendency to make elections conflict generating events, with lots of propaganda, false information, heavy donations, unpolite confrontations, bully fundraising, hostile political parties and organizations, unlimited power ambitions, etc.

This will be completely changed into clean, friendly elections, in which people choose between leaders with outstanding results, plus talent to lead people to peace and freedom, modesty, moderation, good character, friendliness, sharp mind, wisdom, good morals, and intense desire to help people – no campaigning, no publicity, no fundraising, no donations, no debates, no propaganda, no political parties, no advertising, or similar activities.

6.9. All Advisors should also be local Administrators – they must show that they are good managers, and produce practical results for all people.

SUN: Moving to better elections.

EARTH: Yes, and refreshing the management, no propaganda, and produce practical results for all people.
As Hoover said: Freedom is the open window through which pours the sunlight of the human spirit and human dignity.

Finland, Helsinki: the Railway Square, east of the railway station, with the Finnish National Theatre (1872 - 1902).

Japan, Kawaguchi, 17 km north-est of Mount Fuji (3776 m); a big Bonsai tree on the right and three smaller ones on the left.

Proposition 7. World Referendum

7.1 - An electronic world referendum will be organized every three months. The main questions will be:

1. Are you satisfied with the Government?
2. What Government work is good?
3. What Government work is not good?
4: Suggestions for improvement:

7.2 - Within two months after each referendum, the Government will respond to the people. Based on the suggestions received, new pro-people rules will be replacing some old rules.

SUN: An electronic world referendum is refreshing.

EARTH: Certainly, the people will have the opportunity to express their opinions and suggestions.

SUN: When too many incorrect events take place, then what?

EARTH: A change for better becomes inevitable.

UK, Oxford: On Catte Street (to right) at Holywell St (to left), Oxford Martin School (2005, a research and policy unit of the University of Oxford, by James Martin (1933-2013, British information technology consultant and author, worked for IBM, earned a degree in physics at Keble College (1870, by John Keble (1792-1866, English churchman and poet))).

Proposition 8. Complete Disarmament

8.1 - Arms will not exist anymore, and only the police will have some small arms. Those who want arms for hunting or sport, will borrow them from police stations, with proper documents, rules and payments.

8.2 - All military units will become strong civilian organizations, working to improve the quality of life for everybody.

8.3 - For practical reasons, the transition from the current imperfect situation to the much better Sustainable Peace and Prosperity Structure (SPPS) will be very smooth: first - all the countries remain as they are, and they will begin – for example on January 1st, 2021 - to negotiate total and complete disarmament, with the help of the United Nations, for 3 months. Then for 5 months will intensely work to eliminate all the arms – either transform them in peaceful tools, or destroy them. Then a continuous verification and monitoring will be implemented, the make sure that the world finally achieved complete disarmament forever!

SUN: An old dream will finally become realty.

EARTH: Exactly so - arms will not exist anymore, and all military units will become strong civilian organizations. We remember Edison: I am proud of the fact that I never invented weapons to kill.

UK, London: From a bus on Great George St, looking south to the north side of St Margaret's Church (1523), and in the back the eastern part of the north facade and entrance of Westminster Abbey (960, 1517, nave width 26 m, floor area 3,000 m^2, 2 towers, tower height 69 m, 10 bells, church of England, daily services, hosting all English and British coronations since 1066, and 16 royal weddings (from 1100 to 2011); it has the tomb of King Henry III of England (1207-1272).

Proposition 9. Census every 5 years

A census will take place every 5 years – starting, for example, on October 1st, 2023 - and all people will receive a special credit card (SCC), with their photo and other personal data. The delimitations between regions, and between sub-regions, will be adjusted by the census.

SUN: Simple and elegant.

EARTH: Every 5 years we'll know better the world population. Now, the biggest countries by population are: 1 China (1,433 Millions). 2 India (1,366 M), 3 United States (330 M), 4 Indonesia (270 M), 5 Pakistan (216 M), 6 Brazil (211 M), 7 Nigeria (200 M), 8 Bangladesh (163 M), 9 Russia (145 M), 10 Mexico (127 M).
Between the smallest countries by population are: 233 (smallest) Vatican City (799), 217 San Marino (33,860), 216 Liechtenstein (38,019), 214 Monaco (38,964), 203 Andorra (77,142).

Italy, Venezia - The south end of La Piazzetta, the south part of Piazza San Marco, with gondole, and a wedding picture of a Japanese couple.

UK, London: From the northeast corner of Trafalgar Square looking west to the southeast façade of The National Gallery (1824, 2,300 paintings).

Finland, Helsinki: a tall ship in the tourist harbor, in the south-east part of the city.

Washington, DC (1790): the entrance to the Smithsonian Institution Building (1849-1855), on Jefferson Drive SW.

Proposition 10. Special Credit Card (SCC)

The special credit card (SCC) will be used to buy everything, to identify for voting, for census, for travel, for medical assistance, etc.

The current private credit cards will continue to work as usual.

The changes of the delimitations between regions, and also sub-regions, will be inputted on these cards, and no other work is needed.

SUN: Important new idea.

EARTH: The special credit card (SCC) will be much more than a credit card, and will simplify life for everybody.

SUN: Tempora mutantur, et nos mutamur in illis.

EARTH: The times are changing, and we are changing with them

Rome, Vatican, Piazza San Pietro (1667, by Gian Lorenzo Bernini): Basilica di San Pietro (1506, center back), granite fountain by Carlo Maderno (1614, center, north side of piazza).

Finland, Helsinki: the square near a harbor, with the Presidential Palace, the City Hall and other government buildings on the right

Proposition 11. People are something sacred for people

The enemies of the people on Earth are not other people, but viruses, microbes, bad bacteria and hundreds of deadly illnesses – all people on Earth will work together against these real enemies for all of us.

SUN: What a beautiful idea?

EARTH: I love it – of course people are something sacred for people, and all people on Earth will work together against viruses, microbes, bad bacteria and hundreds of deadly illnesses.

SUN: Tell me again what the people really want.

EARTH: All people on the planet want peace, freedom and prosperity, and everybody knows very well that nobody will be able to stop the over 7.7 B people to have what they want: peace, freedom and prosperity. This will be achieved with calm, friendliness and harmony (not with war and violence) in a short period of time, with the help of very wise, peaceful and welcoming leaders.

SUN: Remember Reagan?

EARTH: But of course: No mother would ever willingly sacrifice her sons for territorial gain, for economic advantage, for ideology.

Japan, Mount Fuji (Fuji-san, 3776 m), seen from Fujiyoshida, circa 15 km north-est from Mount Fuji, 1000 m altitude.

Rome: residential apartments near Via Aurelia (constructed around 241 BC by C. Aurelius Cotta, who was a censor) and Piazza Irnerio, about 9 km east of Trajan's Column (113 AD).

Proposition 12. Non-violence and medical assistance

12.1 - Non-violence is a strict requirement for all activities on Earth.

12.2 - The first rule for everybody on Earth comes from the Hippocratic Oath: Primum non nocere - first do not harm.

12.3 - Medical doctors and assistants will make regular home visits to all people, to keep them healthy, and to prevent illnesses.

SUN: This is fundamental. Remember Edison?

EARTH: Sure: Non-violence leads to the highest ethics, which is the goal of all evolution.

Also, all the people will know that doctors will visit them, and help them to stay healthy and happy. The idea is to prevent diseases.

UK, Cambridge: From Trinity Lane looking south to the west part of the northern façade and entrance of King's College Chapel (1446, center back, the College was founded in 1441, and the Old Schools was part of King's College), the east gate of Clare College (1326, as University Hall, making it the second-oldest college of the University, after Peterhouse (1284)) and its Chapel (1763, center right), and the Old Schools (1441, University Offices, left).

Proposition 13. Truth only and collaboration

13.1 - People need only truth in order to create a long term peaceful and harmonious society.

13.2 - If someone lies – medical treatment will follow.

SUN: Hard work will be needed.

EARTH: True, but, step by step, cu calm and patience, the truth will win, simply because it is much better than any lie.
Giordano Bruno: Truth does not change because it is, or is not, believed by a majority of the people.
Cicero: Nature has planted in our minds an insatiable longing to see the truth.
Cicero: Faithfulness and truth are the most sacred excellences and endowments of the human mind.
Goethe: Wisdom is found only in truth.
Rousseau: Falsehood has an infinity of combinations, but truth has only one mode of being.
Aeschylus: In war, truth is the first casualty.
Churchill: A lie gets halfway around the world before the truth has a chance to get its pants on.

UK, Oxford: From the Logic Ln, looking north to the High St and the south gate of the Queen's College (1341, founded by Robert de Eglesfield (1295-1349, chaplain of the Queen consort) in honor of Queen consort Philippa of Hainault (1314-1369, wife of Edward III of England (1312-1377, Reign 1327-1377, burial Westminster Abbey, they had 13 children, and their great-grandfather was King Philip III of France (1245-1285, reign 1270-1285))), University College (1249, left).

Proposition 14. Freedom is required

14.1 - Freedom is a fundamental requirement on Earth.

14.2 - It is well understood that this freedom refers to doing good things in a civilized manner, not for war, violence or similar bad things, which are against the wellbeing of the people.

14.3 - Freedom goes hand in hand with responsibility.

14.4 - People can assemble peacefully only.

14.5 - For economy it is clear that the free market economy, while not perfect, gives the best results, but all people will have the option to choose between friendly private services, and friendly government services. Independent assistants and monitors will make sure that there are no abuses. Sine qua non requirements for happiness are morality and free market.

14.6 - The religion should be free, and is expected not to interfere with activities of the Advisors, and actually should help people.

14.7 - People of course can petition the small Word Government, and can change it anytime, if it does not perform as expected.

SUN: Not so easy job…

EARTH: Sure, we need calm, patience, constant discussions, and wise leaders, with the courage to change some old habits, and move happily to freedom, free markets, and people-oriented decisions.
Thucydides: The secret to happiness is freedom... And the secret to freedom is courage.

Epictetus: Freedom is not procured by a full enjoyment of what is desired, but by controlling the desire.

Finland, Helsinki: the Railway Square, east of the railway station, the bus station (left) and the Finnish National Theatre (center-left).

Proposition 15. Spending less than revenue

All budgets will have surplus of 2% - there will be a strict application of the Latin aphorism: "Sumptus censum ne superset" (Let not your spending exceed your income).

SUN: Actually, there are a few countries which have balanced budgets.

EARTH: Yes, they will be a good example, and, not having war-related expenses, it would much easier to balance the world budgets, and even have a surplus of 2%.

SUN: How do the people react to the huge war-related expenses?

EARTH: The people on the planet brushed off the war preparations and propaganda, and continue to insist on having peace, freedom, good health, good education, and prosperity.

Proposition 16. Correcting errors

16.1 - Correcting errors is a permanent duty for everybody - Darwin (circa 140 years ago) said "To kill an error is as good a service as, and sometimes even better than, the establishing of a new truth or fact."

SUN: As you know, the world is full of errors.

EARTH: Yes, they accumulated over the years, and a good effort will be necessary to correct them all, but it will be done relatively fast.

Japan, Nagoya: a tall building seen from Shinkansen (the bullet train, 320 km/h, started in 1964),

Proposition 17. Kindness is a necessity

Kindness is a requirement for everybody.

Seneca (circa 1,960 years ago) said "Wherever there is a human being, there is an opportunity for a kindness."

This is a fundamental idea which must be constantly applied.

SUN: Seneca said it right.

EARTH: And we all will follow his good advice, because, clearly, it is for the benefit of all of us.

Finland, Helsinki: in the south of the Railway Square is the Ateneum (1887, a major museum of classical art).

UK, Oxford: On St Aldate's St, 200 m north of Broad Walk, 80 m east of Pembroke College, Tom Tower (1682, bell (Great Tom, rung 101 times (every 12 seconds, it takes 20 minutes) at 9 PM every night) tower) over Tom Gate, the main entrance to the majestic Christ Church College (1546, 431 undergraduates, 250 postgraduates, the second wealthiest Oxford college (after St John's), produced 13 British prime ministers), leads into its grand Tom Quad (inside).

Proposition 18. Government mobility

18.1 - All levels of government will be highly mobile - changing of the capitals for the 10 regions, and for the 100 sub-regions, etc.

18.2 - It is necessary to move the government close to the people, to be able to quickly solve the local problems.

18.3 - Locally the people will decide how to better organize themselves, to be more efficient and harmonious, with the help of the world government when necessary. Like in any big family, there will be differences in organization and management, based on their abilities and objectives, but all must be peaceful and harmonious. Conflicts will be promptly resolved by the medical personnel, police, and other assistants.

SUN: Mobility is actually a pleasant requirement.

EARTH: Certainly, changing capitals, meeting new people, are nice activities, and will also help improve the quality of life for all.

SUN: Remember Confucius?

EARTH: The more man meditates upon good thoughts, the better will be his world, and the world at large.

UK, Cambridge: From Trinity Lane looking southeast to the west façade with the entrance to the Old Schools (1441, University Offices, the administrative center of the university, surrounded to the north by Gonville and Caius College (1348), to the east by the University of Cambridge Senate House (1722, where degree ceremonies are held, on King's Parade), to the south by the King's College Chapel (1446), and to the west by Trinity Hall (1350) and Clare College (1326)).

Proposition 19. World Police and Assistance

19.1 - The United Nations will change in 2-3 years (for example, by 2024) into World Police and Assistance Organization (WPAO), to help local police in case of big natural disasters or big accidents, and will report to the top 10 Advisers. They will be located in all capitals, and help the locals. When an emergency appears, they will quickly move to solve the emergency.

19.2 - The police powers will be limited, and they will know and be friend with all the people in their jurisdiction – this is the key element of a civilized and peaceful Earth. If they notice a person with bad intentions, they immediately retain that person and call for a medical assistant (and other assistants, if necessary), to analyze and solve the issue very quickly.

19.3 - Police will be people's friends everywhere, and they will always help people.

19.4 - Prevention of bad events is the main objective of everybody. If a bad event occurs, the police and their assistants will eliminate the consequences, reestablish the normal situation, and determine why the bad event occurred, in order to improve their activity, and prevent such bad events in the future.

19.5 - Private property cannot be taken for public use, without just compensation, decided by at least 5 assistants.

19.6 - A person cannot be deprived by government of life, liberty, or property, without having several doctors and other assistants agree: for life – at least 12; for liberty – at least 6; for property – at least 3.

19.7 - A person cannot deprive another person of life, liberty, or property, which, unfortunately, occurs very frequently in the world, and very much effort and energy will be allocated to prevent such bad events.

19.8 - In order to prevent bad things, the police, doctors and their assistants will be in permanent contact with all the people, by visiting them, phone calls, e-mails, tele-videos, and mail, to keep everybody calm and happy.

SUN: These are serious and demanding issues.

EARTH: Yes:
- The World Police and Assistance Organization (WPAO) will help local police in case of big natural disasters or big accidents, and will report to the top 10 Advisers.
- The police powers will be limited, and they will know and be friend with all the people in their jurisdiction.
- Police will be people's friends everywhere, and they will always help people.
- Prevention of bad events is the main objective of everybody.
Solon: In giving advice seek to help, not to please, your friend.

Finland, Helsinki: on the west side of the Railway Square there is this beautiful building called Fennia, built in 1899, which was first a hotel, then a restaurant, now is the Casino Grand Helsinki.

Proposition 20. Non-stop working

About 66% of the people of the world are working at any moment. Therefore, non-stop working of all world government departments – especially medical, police, emergency, volunteers – will be carefully organized.

SUN: No question that essential government departments will be non-stop working.

EARTH: Sure, in fact all the departments will have employees working anytime somewhere in the world, but the essential government departments will be in all places non-stop working.

SUN: If people have questions, what they do?

EARTH: First ask around, maybe somebody can respond. If not, the government will have a phone and e-mail for questions, and in 3 days they will send a response. This is fundamental – the government will always be ready to respond and help people.
All the public work is Not for me, not for you, but for us – from Latin: Non mihi, non tibi, sed nobis.

Proposition 21. Privacy of discussions

21.1 - In order to have serious and constructive discussions and negotiations, they must be private.

21.2 - Privacy and discipline are necessary for good government work.

21.3 - The results will be public and preserved, but not the private discussions.

SUN: Without privacy, not much can be accomplished.

EARTH: Indeed, private serious discussions, with fast and good results, will be the norm.
Vegetius: Few men are born brave. Many become so through training and force of discipline.

UK, Oxford: On Oriel Street, looking southeast to the west façade of Oriel College (1326), Merton St, Corpus Christy College (1517, right).

Proposition 22. Polite and harmonious government

22.1 - It is a strict requirement for the top management, and for all others, to be highly civilized, polite, courteous, harmonious and efficient.

22.2 - Who wants to work for the world government must have good manners.

22.3 - Harmony in the world starts from the harmony and good manners of the people in the world government.

SUN: Beautiful requirement...

EARTH: The government must be an example in good manners: highly civilized, polite, courteous, harmonious and efficient.
Churchill: It`s not enough that we do our best; sometimes we have to do what`s required.

UK, Oxford: On St Aldate's St, 140 m north of Tom Tower, the south side and entrance (right) of the Museum of Oxford (1975, in the former premises of the Oxford Public Library), a history museum of the City and University of Oxford, from prehistoric times onwards, with original artifacts, Roman pottery, details about King Charles I of England (1600-1649, king 1625-1649, who had Oxford as his stronghold), Oliver Cromwell (1599-1658), etc.

Proposition 23. Transformation in friendship

23.1 - All conflicts must not only be quickly resolved, but they must be transformed in friendships. This is very important for long term stability.

23.2 - The medical personnel and others will work diligently to make sure that disputes are resolved, and then a friendship is developed. Only in this way the situation will become stable.

23.3 - People want peace, freedom, health, friendship and prosperity, therefore conflicts should be quickly resolved, and then the corrective medical treatment will include the transformation of hostility and aggressiveness into harmony and friendship.

SUN: This is a demanding task.

EARTH: Right, but it will be done by talented doctors, who will work with patients until the results are satisfactory.
Newton said: Men build too many walls and not enough bridges.

Finland, Helsinki: the square near the passenger harbor (left), with the Presidential Palace, the City Hall and other government buildings on the right.

Japan, Mount Fuji (3776 m) seen from 12 km north-east, on Higashi-Fuji-Goko Road, in Fujiyoshida; the road 701 to Fuji

Proposition 24. Easy Communication

24.1 - As a single big, over 7.7 B, family on Earth, all people must be able to communicate easily with each other.

24.2 - For this reason, a common language and alphabet on Earth are needed. Because English is a de facto common language now, it will be taken as the basis of the world language, let's call it Mundo, which will be taught in all schools, and used in the world government. All the other languages will continue as secondary languages.

24.3 - The same is true for the Latin alphabet, which will be used everywhere, with other alphabets as secondary.

24.4 - The teachers will have a very significant role in implementing this proposition.

SUN: Easy communication requires very hard work.

EARTH: Absolutely, but it is very important. You see, having hundreds of languages and dialects, and several alphabets, does not help to come together as a big family. Many people already know some English and the Latin alphabet, therefore, with the help of talented teachers, all will be able to learn the common language (English-based) Mundo. Then, obviously, the things will get much better.

UK, Oxford: On Merton Street an entrance to Corpus Christy College (1517, founder Richard Foxe, the Bishop of Winchester, 12th oldest college in Oxford (1st University College (1249, 2nd Balliol College (1263), 3rd Merton College (1264)), 249 undergraduates, 94 postgraduates), situated between Merton College (1264, founded by Walter de Merton (1205-1277), Lord Chancellor to Henry III (1207-1272) and later to Edward I (1239-1307), and Catholic Bishop of Rochester (1274-1277); Merton College Library (1373) is the oldest functioning library in the world), and Oriel College (1326).

Proposition 25. Global wealth for Peace only

25.1 - The 2018 Global Wealth Report from Credit Suisse shows that the total global wealth has reached $317 trillions (circa $41,000/person), which is encouraging, and all this wealth must be used only for peace.

25.2 - Like in any big family, there are differences, because some work more, some spend less, some move faster, and, especially, some are sick – this is the main reason for differences: not all people can be equally sick, some people are sicker than others. However, all the people and the government will work to help each other.

25.3 - It is a major responsibility of the Government to increase the global wealth, and to train those in need to have better working abilities and opportunities.

SUN: Really good points we have here.

EARTH: Yes, wealth is important, all the people and the government will work to help each other, and to train those in need to have better working abilities and opportunities.

Finland, Helsinki: the central part of the Ateneum (1885 - 1887, a major museum of classical art). Up is a phrase in Latin: Concordia res parvae crescund (By unity small states flourish). The four caryatids represent architecture, painting, music and sculpting.

Proposition 26. No bureaucracy

26.1 - No bureaucracy – this is required by all people, and every day attention will be given for improvements in this direction.

26.2 - In a well-organized country, with all people working together in harmony, this can be accomplished in several years.

SUN: No bureaucracy is a nice dream.

EARTH: We want this dream to became reality – not over night, but working every day, for a few years, with patience and perseverance, it will be accomplished.

Reagan: No government ever voluntarily reduces itself in size. Government programs, once launched, never disappear. Actually, a government bureau is the nearest thing to eternal life we'll ever see on this earth!

Japan, Lake Kawaguchi (17 km north-est of Mount Fuji), 833 m altitude, 15 m depth, 19 km shore length, 6.13 km^2, in the morning

Proposition 27. No corruption, no duplication

27.1 - Everybody will work really hard to completely eliminate corruption, organized crime and drug trafficking.

27.2 - Constant attention will be focused on avoiding duplication at all levels of the world government – there must be continuous collaboration between all levels, to prevent duplication, and to eliminate it, if it was found.

A vice is nourished by being concealed (from Latin: Alitur vitium vivitque tegendo

SUN: All are big tasks.

EARTH: Certainly, but calm, friendly and well-organized effort, involving also medical personnel and police, will finally eliminate these problems. The idea is that nothing is impossible, if the people really want to do it.

Washington, D.C. (1790): George Washington (1732-1799, first President 1789-1797) Monument (1848-1885, 169 m, 43 ha), on the National Mall, 700 m south of the White House, seen from the Constitution Avenue NW.

Italy, Rome. Isola Tiberina in the middle of Tiber river, which flows to the back, viewed from Ponte Garibaldi (1888), with Pons Cestius (27 BC, the first stone bridge, right, connecting Isola Tiberina with Trastevere).

Proposition 28. World reserve system

28.1 - Each government department will have some reserves for special situations (natural disasters, big accidents), and the banks will also have good financial reserves.

28.2 - All people will be encouraged to save some money in banks with 5% interest.

SUN: Reserves and savings are important.

EARTH: Yes, and here will have some changes – you see, everybody needs to have some government guaranteed savings in banks, with 5% interest. The future is not in betting on horses, or athletes, or companies, which all can be easily manipulated, but in saving from your own hard work. Playing cards, or lottery, or stocks is not good.

SUN: Vitam mutaveris in meliores actus.

EARTH: Change your life for the better.

UK, Oxford: From Merton Street, looking southeast to the north (left) and west (right) facades of Merton College Chapel (1294, 1425, 1451, the church of Merton College (1264, the third oldest in Oxford)); there were plans to extend this church to the west (right), but the land was leased in 1517 to Bishop Richard Foxe (1448-1528), who founded Corpus Christy College (1517), next door (west) to Merton.

Proposition 29. Integrity and efficiency

29.1 - Inspectors will help the Government with the integrity and efficiency issues – always there are ways to improve the work.

29.2 - Inspectors will give advice regarding integrity and efficiency, and will take corrective actions when necessary.

SUN: Always there is room for improvement in these areas.

EARTH: Sure, for this the friendly inspectors will help with advices and big smiles.
Leonardo da Vinci: Nothing strengthens authority so much as silence.

Japan, Nagoya: tall buildings seen from Shinkansen (the bullet train, 320 km/h, started in 1964),

Finland, Helsinki: The Three smiths statue (by Felix Nylund, 1932), with the Old Student House (1870, left) and Tallberg's house (right). On the base: MONUMENTUM – CURAVIT – LEGATUM – J. TALLBERGIANUM – PRO HELSINGFORS A.D. MCMXXXII ("The statue was erected with the help of a donation from J. Tallberg by Pro Helsingfors in the year 1932").

UK, Oxford: From Broad St, looking southeast to the north façade of Clarendon Building, the registration ceremony at the University of Oxford.

Proposition 30. Family assistance

Because all families need assistance from time to time, and the big 7.7 B family on Earth contains billions of small families, all of them will have the assistance they need – this will be the result of one country well organized and managed.

SUN: There are over 2 billions of families in the world.

EARTH: Yes, and all of them will be the focus of the world government – and each of these families will live in peace, freedom and prosperity.

SUN: Remember Homer, over 2,800 years ago?

EARTH: Certainly: There is nothing nobler or more admirable than when a man and a woman, who see eye to eye, keep house as man and wife, confounding their enemies, and delighting their friends.

Japan, Mount Fuji (Fuji-san, 3776 m), seen in the morning from the window of a hotel in Kawaguchi, circa 17 km north-est.

Finland, Helsinki: the north-east side of the Railway Square, with the Radisson Blu Plaza Hotel Helsinki (center-left) and the Casino Helsinki (right). In winter time, the Railway Square hosts an ice-skating rink and the people from Casino and from hotel enjoy skating just near the door. It seems that the earliest ice skating happened in southern Finland, maybe around this place, more than 3000 years ago.

Proposition 31. Living in harmony

Because all people on Earth want to live in harmony right now, it will be relatively easy to implement this in one good and civilized country. This may include having small, beautiful and commonly agreed fences around properties, because good fences make good neighbors, and also helps with more privacy.

SUN: Harmony, like in music, is so important…

EARTH: And we will finally have it, when we'll implement the world constitution.

The first rule for everybody on Earth comes from the Hippocratic Oath: Primum non nocere - first do not harm.

Japan, Yamatokoriyama, rural scene seen from Shinkansen (the bullet train, 320 km/h, started in 1964).

Proposition 32. Dispute resolution

32.1 - Dispute resolution is not only Government's obligation, but it will be everybody's duty.

32.2 - There will be professional assistance from medical personnel, police, people assistance specialists, volunteers, religious organizations, and many others, but the bottom line is that everybody must avoid disputes.

32.3 - When there are different opinions, just stay calm, express your opinion, listen to others, and continue calm the discussion until a compromise is reached.

32.4 – There is no need to spend much time and energy – let the people decide, and even if your idea is not temporarily accepted, there are chances that in the future you'll have more people agree with you.

SUN: Avoiding disputes is a good objective.

EARTH: Sure, nobody is right all the time, therefore everybody will accept new and constructive ideas, which will have practical benefits for all.
Let us refrain from erring – from Latin: Festinamus errare.
To err is human, to persevere is of the devil – from Latin: Errare humanum est, perseverare diabolicum.

Finland, Helsinki: trams (first appeared in 1807 in UK) on Mannerheimintie.

Rome. Down: a part of Forum Augustum (2 BC). Back: a part of Forum Traiani (113 AD), including the Columna Traiani (113, center back).

Proposition 33. No abuses

33.1 - Special attention will be given by Advisors to avoid abuses and wrong interpretations of the rules. All assistants (doctors, mathematicians, CEOs, engineers and teachers) will closely monitor all activities, to avoid abuses and wrong interpretations of the rules.

33.2 - This requirement of not having abuses is demanding – but this is a general job, not only for Government, but for everybody, as part of the big family, we just don't need abuses.

33.3 - The abuse, in some places, of confiscating the land by some government bureaucrats will be eliminated – the land belongs to the people, not the government.

33.4 - The abuse, in some places, of having trains, airplanes, and others making unhealthy noises, with the government support, will be eliminated – peoples' health has always priority.

33.5 – The abuse, in some places, of having to change the clocks twice a year will be eliminated – only the normal local time zones will be used.

33.6 - If abuses are observed, they will be immediately reported to the Government, and corrected, in general, by the People Assistance Department, which will have personnel, including medical assistants, to analyze and promptly solve the abuses.

SUN: Abuses are relatively frequent…

EARTH: Yes, unfortunately, and will require some extra attention from the government, and from all people. The abuse of naming hurricanes with people's names will be eliminated, wasting people's money on unnecessary projects must go, and many others. Step by step, it will be done.

USA, New York (1624): on 42nd street, close to 8th Avenue, inside a tall building, three sculptures of people waiting at a door.

Japan, Kyoto, Kyoto Century Hotel, 10 km north-west of Byodo-in Temple (998), seen from Shinkansen (the bullet train, 320 km/h).

Proposition 34. Free commerce

34.1 - In one country, with one market, the commerce between the people on Earth will be free of taxes, tariffs, duties, etc. – plenty of opportunities for everybody.

34.2 - The speech will be free and responsible. It is expected not to call for war, violence, or similar destructive activities. People want peace, freedom, health, friendship and prosperity.

34.3 - The press will be free and responsible. It is expected not to call for war, violence, or similar destructive activities. People want peace, freedom, health, friendship and prosperity.

34.4 - People can assemble peacefully only, with police for help. It is expected not to call for war, violence, or similar destructive activities. People want peace, freedom, health, friendship and prosperity.

SUN: Freedom, of course, goes hand in hand with responsibility.

EARTH: Exactly, and the most important freedom is to quietly elect new world government leaders every 20 months, and to have referendums on their work every 3 months.

SUN: Cicero said it nicely….

EARTH: Freedom is a possession of inestimable value.

Finland, Helsinki: commercial buildings south (left) and west (center) of Helsinki Central Railway Station (1907 – 1914).

UK, Oxford: On Merton St. at Magpie Lane (to right, to Old Bank Hotel), looking west to the south part of Oriel College (1326).

Proposition 35. Jobs for all

35.1 - There will always be plenty of jobs at world minimum wage (assisting other people, for example), and the standard situation will be this: more jobs than available people, so people will choose the jobs they like the most.

35.2 - No unemployment, no homelessness, no begging – just all working harmoniously, having good houses, and helping each other.

SUN: This is definitely a big success.

EARTH: Certainly, everybody will have a free e-mail from the government, in addition to private e-mails, to be able to freely communicate, find jobs, etc., without any advertisements. Having a job which you like is really important.

UK, Cambridge: From Trinity Ln, looking west through the entrance of Trinity Hall, (1350, by William Baterman (c 1298-1355, Bishop of Norwich between 1344 and 1355), a constituent college (the 5th oldest) of the University of Cambridge), to the Front Court and the entrance to the west building of the Front Court. To the northeast of Trinity Hall there is the separate Trinity College (1546, founder Henry VIII (1491-1547, reign 1509-1547), motto: Virtus Vera Nobilitas).

Proposition 36. Limited number of rules

36.1 - All rules proposed by Advisers must be approved by their 5 assistants (doctors, mathematicians, CEOs, engineers and teachers), and for any new rule over 2,000 basic rules (each rule on at most half a page, total 1,000 pages), at least on old rule must be eliminated.

36.2 - All the rules can be changed or eliminated when a majority of the people or their Advisors agree, but some fundamental peace and order rules will remain.

SUN: Good and refreshing idea.

EARTH: After a number of years, when all the people on the planet will be highly civilized, friendly and respectful, no rules will be needed, because everybody will know from schools and from experience, how to comport themselves, and how to work together for the benefit of all.

Proposition 37. Constitution improvements

This Constitution of the World can be improved when 66% of the voters agree.

SUN: This Constitution of the World is very good indeed, but always there is room for improvement.

EARTH: After much more experience is accumulated as a single country on the planet, there will be new ideas to be added, which will make the life even better for all.

UK, Oxford: From the main entrance, looking east to the east side of the Front quad (the oldest collegiate quadrangle) of Merton College (1264)

Proposition 38. General ideas

38.1 - The purpose for all people on Earth is to be healthy, to live in peace, freedom and harmony, to be prosperous, and to prepare to expand to the Moon, asteroids, Mars, and other places in the Universe, which can support life.

SUN: This purpose is excellent.

EARTH: I can't wait to get there! Especially having people from Earth living on the Moon, asteroids, Mars, and other places in the Universe, which can support life, is absolutely fantastic!

38.2 - Important immediate objectives for everybody are:
- Reserve time for happiness.
- Use robots and automated processes, work less, and spend more time with your family.
- The weekend will be like a small vacation.
- Prevent burnout.
- Make civilized behavior and harmony everywhere an important issue.
- Eliminate stress.
- Help friends and colleagues.
- Keep everybody relaxed, calm, friendly, patient, and happy.

38.3 - To start this new structure of the world, one idea could be this: the first Honorific World Observer (from UN, for example) could invite 10 Presidents form big countries (like USA, China, Russia, UK, India, France, Japan, Germany, Brasil, and Egypt) to be the first 10 Advisors Level 4, starting, for example, on January 1st, 2021, for 10 months, until November 1st, 2021, when the new calm and noiseless elections will take place. The same for the 100 Advisers Level 3, and so on.

38.4 - For better understanding and easier implementation of this Constitution, the following books, by Michael M. Dediu, are recommended:

- Our Future is Sustainable Peace and Prosperity – Moving from conflicts to harmony and peace

– Our Future Depends on Good World Educations – Moving from frail education to solid education.

– Friendly, Helpful & Smart World Management - Moving from bureaucracy to responsive world management

– If You Want Peace, Prepare for Peace! – Moving from preparation for war to preparation for peace

– World with One Country & its Ten Friendly Regions - Moving from 195 disagreeing countries, to 1 country with 10 collaborating regions

– After 10,000 Years of Conflicts, People want 10,000 Years of Harmony - Moving from continuous wars to stable peace

SUN: Now we can add more recommendations.

EARTH: Yes, these two new books:

- World Constitution Implementation – Moving from violent changes, to smooth transition to the Constitution of the World

- It is getting truer and truer – we urgently need the World Constitution: Moving from anarchic changes, to balanced transition to the Constitution of the World

There are also 44 Dediu Newsletters – World Monthly Reports, with very interesting and useful information.

UK, Oxford: From Merton St. looking south to the northern façade of the main entrance of Merton College (1264). Important personalities associated with Merton College are British chemist Frederick Soddy (1877-1956, Nobel Prize in Chemistry (1921)), poet T. S. Elliot (1888 in St Louis, U. S. – 1965 in London, England, Nobel Prize in Literature (1948)), British philosopher John R. Lucas (born 1932), British mathematician Sir Andrew Wiles (born 1953, proved Fermat's (1607-1665) Last Theorem (1637) proved after 358 years).

Proposition 39. Extensions

This Constitution of the World is valid not only on Earth, but also on the space around Earth, on the Moon, Mars, asteroids and any other places were the very good people on Earth will be moving in the future.

SUN: This is a big joy – peace everywhere!

EARTH: And freedom, and prosperity – what do you want more?!

USA, Boston (founded in 1630): visiting tall ships from many countries, at the Boston Fish Pier (opened in 1915).

Proposition 40. Intentions and putting into practice

40-1 - This Constitution of the World is intended for at least 10,000 years of harmonious living on the happy Earth.

40.2 – The present Constitution of the World is ready to come into force, and to be put into practice, for the benefit of all people on Earth, on 6 March 2020, and it is ready to remain into force, and enjoyed by all people, at least until 6 March 12020.

SUN: Astonishing – let's do it!

EARTH: We are working on it right now, and we'll succeed really soon, because, as Victor Hugo said "All the forces in the world are not so powerful as an idea whose time has come".

SUN: The sooner, the better!

Rome. Down: a part of Forum Augustum (2 BC). Back: a part of Forum Traiani (113 AD), including Columna Traiani (113, center back), with a band (180 m) of carved reliefs, which winds around the Trajan's Column, describing Trajan's Dacian war campaigns (101-102 and 105-106 AD). After Trajan's death, his 6 m statue was on top until 1587. His ashes and later those of his wife Plotina were placed in the base of the column.